Football Club

ESTᴰ 1879

This Annual belongs to

Age

Favourite player

Prediction of Fulham's final position this season

Prediction of Sky Bet Championship winners this season

Prediction of FA Cup winners this season

Prediction of Capital One Cup winners this season

Prediction of teams to be promoted
to the Barclays Premier League this season:

1st

2nd

Play Off Winners

Written by twocan
Contributor: Rob Mason

A TWOCAN PUBLICATION

©2014. Published by twocan
under licence from Fulham Football Club.

ISBN 978-1-909872-22-6

£8

Fulham Football Club
ESTD 1879

Being a striker has its rewards...

Fulham Football Club
ESTD 1879

BARRY HAYLES

LOUIS SAHA

...but it's more about guts than glory!

TOP 10 STRIKING TIPS

You have to put in the legwork to reap the benefits so here we give you some top tips for becoming a striker supreme.

1 WORK HARD!
Play your heart out right up until the final whistle, you never know when that perfect cross will come your way.

2 PASS THE BALL!
The object is for the team to score, not the individual, if someone else has a better opportunity, help them to take it.

3 DON'T SACRIFICE ACCURACY FOR POWER!
No matter how hard you kick the ball, if a shot isn't on target, it's never going in.

4 FOLLOW THROUGH!
Strike the ball with the laces of your boot and don't stop your leg motion once you've connected with the ball. If you swing your leg through it will give you more momentum.

5 KEEP SHOTS LOW AND AIM FOR THE CORNERS!
These are the hardest areas for the goalie to protect.

6 PRACTISE MAKES PERFECT!
Practise shooting at a small target like a pole or tree to improve your accuracy, you can gradually increase your distance from the object. Soon you'll be scoring from 25 yards!

7 ATTACK AT EVERY CHANCE YOU GET!
Make the defensive team work, the more shots you have on target, the more likely you are to score.

8 BE PATIENT!
Don't just shoot because the ball's at your feet, wait for chances, don't waste them.

9 WORK ON BOTH FEET!
Practise shooting with both feet, your weaker foot as well as your stronger. This will help make you a better all-round player. The more skilled you are, the more opportunities will present themselves.

10 HAVE CONFIDENCE IN YOURSELF!
If you get a chance, take it. If you think you can take your defender on, go for it! Think fast and be decisive if you want to out-fox your opponent.

Louis SAHA

2000-2004

'King Louis' joined Fulham from Metz for £2.1m in 2000, and went on to score 63 goals in 142 appearances for the Whites.

Saha was known for his superb pace, strength and shooting power, and formed a formidable partnership with Louis Boa Morte and Barry Hayles in the 2000/01 season where we won promotion to the Premiership. That season, Saha's first at Fulham, he scored an impressive 27 league goals and from there he never looked back: he scored twice in Fulham's first-ever Premiership game, in an agonising but heroic 3-2 defeat to then-champions Manchester United, who he would move to in a £12.3m deal in 2004.

Saha continued his rich vein of form in the Premiership and terrorised defences for 13 seasons for Fulham, United, Everton, Tottenham Hotspur and Sunderland.

Gordon DAVIES

1978-1984

Where else to start other than that Gordon Davies is Fulham's all-time top goalscorer?

Davies scored 159 goals in 460 appearances over two spells at the Cottage, spending 11 seasons in total on the banks of the Thames - sandwiched around short spells at both Chelsea and Manchester City.

Known affectionately as 'Ivor' due to the Welsh international sounding a lot like TV's Ivor the Engine, Davies is still a hugely popular figure amongst Fulham fans young and old.

Brian McBRIDE

2004-2008

The all-American hero, Brian McBride led the Fulham line as Club Captain and with pure guts, drive and determination.

In the five seasons he spent at Fulham he scored 41 goals and you will struggle to find someone who can head a ball better! A truly fearless player, McBride would always work his socks off for the team and his return from injury in the 2007/08 'Great Escape' season was a key factor in Fulham avoiding relegation. He scored in victories over Reading and Birmingham City, two sides who were relegated beneath the Whites on the final day of the season.

HONOURABLE MENTIONS: Barry Hayles, Geoff Horsefield, Frank 'Bonzo' Newton, Graham Leggat, Bobby Zamora

Tim HOOGLAND

2

Fulham
Football Club
ESTD 1879

Set up three cones in a large triangle. These become our three goals! Make sure the triangle is big enough for the goalie to dive around in.

The goalie stands in the centre of the triangle and three shooters stand opposite the three goals at their 'penalty spots'.

This drill is very tiring for the keeper. Remember to swap positions so that everyone gets the chance to be in goal.

EASY

To start with, the shooters take it in turns to fire shots past the goalie - the goalie must work quickly to reposition himself for the next shot.

HARD

Players then start to fire shots more quickly. Just as the goalkeeper recovers from the last shot, the next player quickly shoots again.

HARDER

Change the order in which the shooters take their shots. Shooters shout their names in any order, to signal that they are going to shoot.

This keeps the goalie on his toes.

Also, be sure to try different shots - high, low, left foot, right foot, maybe even try chipping the ball over the keeper's head!

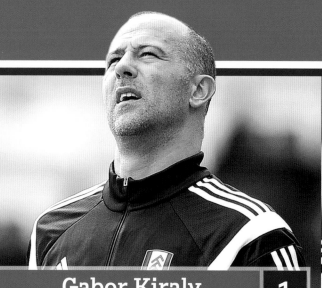

Gabor Kiraly — 1

POSITION: Goalkeeper

NATIONALITY: Hungarian **DOB:** 1 April 1976

DID YOU KNOW? Since making his international debut against Austria in 1998, he has amassed 90 caps for his country. In a senior career which started in 1993, the experienced stopper has played 753 professional games.

Tim Hoogland — 2

POSITION: Defender

NATIONALITY: German **DOB:** 11 June 1985

DID YOU KNOW? The German right-back joined the Whites following the expiry of his contract with Bundesliga outfit Schalke 04, and has been capped at U18, U19 and U20 level for the German national team.

THE SQUAD

Shaun Hutchinson — 4

POSITION: Defender

NATIONALITY: English **DOB:** 23 November 1990

DID YOU KNOW? The Newcastle-born defender began his career at Wallsend Boys Club - the Club where players such as Alan Shearer and former Fulham hero Lee Clark started.

Fernando Amorebieta — 5

POSITION: Defender

NATIONALITY: Venezuelan **DOB:** 29 March 1985

DID YOU KNOW? Born in Venezuela, Fernando met former Club Athletic Bilbao's eligibility criteria as he had been raised locally since the age of two, while his parents are also of Basque origin.

Fulham
Football Club
ESTᴰ 1879

'14·15

Konstantinos Stafylidis 3

POSITION: Defender

NATIONALITY: Greek   **DOB:** 2 December 1993

DID YOU KNOW? Born in Thessaloniki, the Greek left-back is on a season-long loan from Bundesliga side Bayer Leverkusen.

Fulham
Football Club
ESTD 1879

THE SQUAD 14-15

Nikolay Bodurov | 6

POSITION: Defender

NATIONALITY: Bulgarian **DOB:** 30 May 1986

DID YOU KNOW? Nikolay plays primarily as a centre-back but can also play on the right side of defence. He earned international acclaim in 2010, when he made his debut against Wales in Cardiff.

Thomas Eisfeld | 7

POSITION: Midfielder

NATIONALITY: German **DOB:** 18 January 1993

DID YOU KNOW? Thomas made two senior appearances for Arsenal. His debut came as a second-half substitute at Reading in the League Cup. Arsenal went on to win 7-5 in extra-time despite trailing 4-0 at the break.

Scott Parker | 8

POSITION: Midfielder

NATIONALITY: English **DOB:** 13 October 1980

DID YOU KNOW? Scott's tough tackling and never-say-die attitude makes him a fans' favourite. He was voted Football Writers' Footballer of the Year in 2011 and captained England the following year.

First team profiles...

Matt Smith | 9

POSITION: Forward

NATIONALITY: English   DOB: 7 June 1989

DID YOU KNOW? Now reunited at Craven Cottage, Matt formed a formidable partnership with Ross McCormack at Leeds United last season, scoring 13 goals in 43 appearances.

Bryan Ruiz | 10

POSITION: Forward

NATIONALITY: Costa Rican   DOB: 18 August 1985

DID YOU KNOW? Bryan captained Costa Rica in their impressive 2014 World Cup campaign and scored the only goal as they upset four-time champions Italy to qualify for the knock-out stage.

Elsad Zverotić | 13

POSITION: Defender

NATIONALITY: Montenegrin   DOB: 31 Oct 1986

DID YOU KNOW? A versatile player who can fit in anywhere in defence or midfield, Elsad is also a Montenegro international who played against England in the 2014 World Cup Qualifying campaign.

Fulham
Football Club
ESTᴰ 1879

THE SQUAD '14-15

Patrick Roberts
14

POSITION: Forward

NATIONALITY: English **DOB:** 5 February 1997

DID YOU KNOW? Patrick played a major role as Fulham U18s reached the FA Youth Cup Final for the first time last season, narrowly missing out 7-6 on aggregate to Chelsea.

14

Kay Voser 15

POSITION: Defender

NATIONALITY: Swiss   DOB: 4 January 1987

DID YOU KNOW? Last season Kay made eight appearances in the UEFA Champions League for FC Basel which included two group match victories against Chelsea.

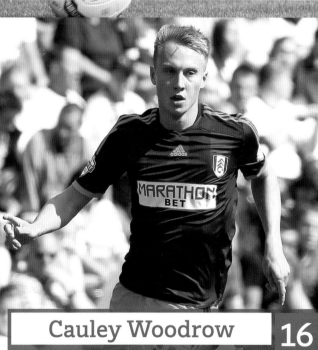

Cauley Woodrow 16

POSITION: Forward

NATIONALITY: English   DOB: 2 December 1994

DID YOU KNOW? Cauley's season finished positively when he scored his first goal for the Club on the final day of the campaign against Crystal Palace, before being called up to the England U21 squad.

Adam Taggart 17

POSITION: Forward

NATIONALITY: Australian   DOB: 2 June 1993

DID YOU KNOW? Adam signed on a three-year deal from Australia A-League side Newcastle Jets, where last season he earned the A-League Golden Boot, A-League Young Footballer of the Year and inclusion into the 2013/14 A-League PFA Team of the Season.

Hugo Rodallega 20

POSITION: Forward

NATIONALITY: Colombian   **DOB:** 25 July 1985

DID YOU KNOW? Hugo began his professional career in his native Colombia with Deportes Quindío where he averaged almost a goal every other game. He also has over 40 caps and has netted eight times for his country.

Dino Fazlic 22

POSITION: Midfielder

NATIONALITY: Bosnian   **DOB:** 21 November 1991

DID YOU KNOW? Dino started at Werder Bremen's youth team before moving to Bolton Wanderers and was signed from Swiss side Grasshopper Club Zurich on a one-year deal in August following a successful trial period.

Lasse Vigen Christensen 21

POSITION: Midfielder

NATIONALITY: Danish   **DOB:** 15 August 1994

DID YOU KNOW? Lasse, a Danish youth international, is creative in possession and is regarded as one of Denmark's most promising young players.

Tiago Casasola 23

POSITION: Defender

NATIONALITY: Argentinian   **DOB:** 11 August 1995

DID YOU KNOW? Tiago, signed from Boca Juniors, has represented Argentina at U20 level and travelled to the 2014 World Cup in Brazil to play against the full national side as part of their preparations for the tournament.

First team profiles...

Moussa Dembélé — 25

POSITION: Forward

NATIONALITY: French **DOB:** 12 July 1996

DID YOU KNOW? Moussa, signed from Paris Saint-Germain, had a fantastic 2013/14 scoring goals for fun at U18 level. His form progressed to the U21 squad and he went on to make three first team appearances.

George Williams — 27

POSITION: Forward

NATIONALITY: Welsh **DOB:** 7 September 1995

DID YOU KNOW? Although George was born in England he is a Welsh international after qualifying to represent the nation through his mother.

Mark Fotheringham — 26

POSITION: Midfielder

NATIONALITY: Scottish **DOB:** 22 October 1983

DID YOU KNOW? Mark, who started his senior career at Celtic, made 21 appearances for Notts County in Sky Bet League One last season. He has bags of experience of domestic and European football, enjoying spells in England, Scotland, Germany, Switzerland and Cyprus.

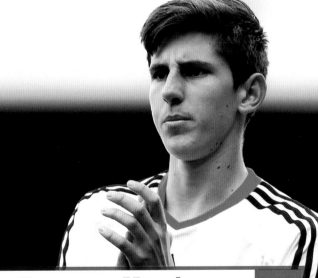

Emerson Hyndman — 28

POSITION: Midfielder

NATIONALITY: American **DOB:** 9 April 1996

DID YOU KNOW? Emerson is a USA international with a great attitude. His impressive performances on the pitch ware rewarded with his first professional contract at Fulham in April 2013 and has signed an extension keeping him at Craven Cottage until 2016.

Chris David   30

POSITION: Midfielder

NATIONALITY: Dutch   DOB: 6 March 1993

DID YOU KNOW? Chris got off the mark for Fulham in spectacular style on the last day of the 2013/14 season when his sumptuous strike in stoppage time earned the Whites a point against Crystal Palace.

Sean Kavanagh   32

POSITION: Defender

NATIONALITY: Irish   DOB: 24 January 1994

DID YOU KNOW? Technically assured, tenacious in the tackle and a fine reader of play, Sean has the ability to deliver pin-point crosses into the box.

Dan Burn   33

POSITION: Defender

NATIONALITY: English   DOB: 9 May 1992

DID YOU KNOW? The towering centre-back made his debut in January 2014 in the FA Cup Third Round tie at Norwich City. He featured heavily for Fulham over the remainder of the season, making nine league appearances in total.

Adil Chihi   34

POSITION: Midfielder

NATIONALITY: Moroccan DOB: 21 February 1988

DID YOU KNOW? Adil previously played for German side FC Cologne, where he had made more than 130 senior appearances and scored 20 goals. Born in Dusseldorf, he is of Moroccan descent and has made two international appearances for their national team.

Cameron Burgess 38

POSITION: Defender

NATIONALITY: Scottish   DOB: 21 October 1995

DID YOU KNOW? Cameron began his football education in Scotland, where he played in the youth teams of both Glasgow Celtic and Aberdeen, before moving with his family to Australia. Cameron is following in his father's and grandfather's footsteps as they both played professional football too.

Marcus Bettinelli 40

POSITION: Goalkeeper

NATIONALITY: English   DOB: 24 May 1992

DID YOU KNOW? Marcus was on loan to Accrington Stanley last term where he impressed as the Lancashire outfit moved clear of the League Two relegation places. His form saw him named Accrington's Young Player of the Season.

Ryan Williams 39

POSITION: Midfielder

NATIONALITY: Australian   DOB: 28 October 1993

DID YOU KNOW? Ryan, born in Subiaco, Australia, is a pacey winger who brings determination and skill, delivering great crosses from either flank.

Jesse Joronen 41

POSITION: Goalkeeper

NATIONALITY: Finnish   DOB: 21 March 1993

DID YOU KNOW? Having worked closely with the young keeper in the past, Antti Niemi has tipped him for the top. In January 2013 he made his full debut for his country in a King's Cup match against Thailand.

Ross McCormack 44

POSITION: Forward

NATIONALITY: Scottish   **DOB:** 18 August 1986

DID YOU KNOW? Signed from Leeds United, Glasgow-born Ross started his career at Rangers, before spells at Motherwell and Cardiff City.

ROSS McCORMACK

TOP 3: Midfielders

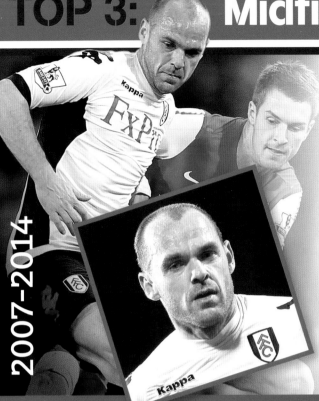

Fulham Football Club
ESTD 1879

2007-2014

Another Fulham Captain, probably best known for the header at Fratton Park which gave the Whites a 1-0 win against Portsmouth on the final day of the 2007/08 season - ensuring our Premier League survival.

The former Liverpool, Charlton Athletic and Tottenham Hotspur midfielder joined on deadline day in summer 2007, and quickly became a key figure in the middle of the park. Murphy's ability to dictate play with his superb range of passing was his greatest asset, as well as being a dead-ball expert and mean penalty taker!

Murphy was virtually ever-present during the famous UEFA Europa League campaign in 2009/2010, where he captained the famous side all the way to the Final.

Danny MURPHY

Johnny HAYNES

'The Maestro' is unquestionably Fulham's greatest-ever player and who Pele described as "the best passer of the ball I've ever seen."

Johnny joined Fulham as a schoolboy in 1952 and would spend 18 years at Craven Cottage - amassing an incredible 594 appearances and 147 goals over that period. Not only that, he also earned 56 caps for England - 22 as captain - and scored 18 goals for the national team. His finest moment came when England thrashed Scotland 9-3 at Wembley in 1961, where Haynes, the captain, scored twice.

When the wage cap in English football was abolished, also in 1961, Haynes became the first £100-a-week player. Following his tragic death in 2005, a statue featuring Haynes in his famous 'hands on hips' pose, was erected outside Craven Cottage on Stevenage Road. The Stevenage Road Stand was also renamed the Johnny Haynes Stand in his honour.

1952-1970

Sean DAVIS

1996-2004

Sean Davis remains the only player to play for Fulham in all four divisions (and hopefully he'll be the last!).

Davis came through the Academy ranks and broke through to the First Team as Fulham stormed up the divisions in the late 90s. The scorer of two of Fulham's most famous goals in recent years, the winner against Blackburn Rovers at Ewood Park, and the equaliser that clinched the Division One title against Sheffield Wednesday (both in the 2000/2001 promotion season), Sean remains a hugely popular figure at Fulham and is still involved at the Club both with media activities and coaching young Academy players at Motspur Park.

HONOURABLE MENTIONS: Lee Clark, Mousa Dembélé, Steed Malbranque, Ray Lewington, Luis Boa Morte

21

Fan'tastic

Fulham
Football Club
ESTD 1879

22

Can you help him?

Using the numbers of the Fulham squad can you work out the answers to the following sums?

For example, Matt Smith is No. 9 and Scott Parker is No. 8 so Matt Smith + Scott Parker is 17.

Bryan Ruiz + Adil Chihi =

Patrick Roberts + Thomas Eisfeld =

Scott Parker − Tim Hoogland =

Jesse Joronen − Hugo Rodallega =

Tim Hoogland X Elsad Zverotic =

Scott Parker X Shaun Hutchinson =

Marcus Bettinelli ÷ Scott Parker =

Ryan Williams ÷ Elsad Zverotic =

1	Gabor Kiraly	21	Lasse Vigen Christensen
2	Tim Hoogland	22	Dino Fazlic
3	Konstantinos Stafylidis	23	Tiago Casasola
4	Shaun Hutchinson	25	Moussa Dembele
5	Fernando Amorebieta	26	Mark Fotheringham
6	Nikolay Bodurov	27	George Williams
7	Thomas Eisfeld	28	Emerson Hyndman
8	Scott Parker	30	Chris David
9	Matt Smith	32	Sean Kavanagh
10	Bryan Ruiz	33	Dan Burn
13	Elsad Zverotic	34	Adil Chihi
14	Patrick Roberts	38	Cameron Burgess
15	Kay Voser	39	Ryan Williams
16	Cauley Woodrow	40	Marcus Bettinelli
17	Adam Taggart	41	Jesse Joronen
20	Hugo Rodallega	44	Ross McCormack

Fulham
Football Club
ESTᴅ 1879

Kay VOSER

15

25

C Born in Sierra Leone, he's played multiple times for England at U21 level

D Exciting young Frenchman signed from Paris Saint-Germain.

E Dutch striker, signed for Swansea in January 2014

STAR STUDDED

A Venezuelan no-nonsense defender signed from Athletic Bilbao.

F Defender, who's at home at the Riverside Stadium

B He has twice won Derby's Player of the Year Award - in 2012 and 2014

G French striker known for his size & physical style of play

Figure out who's who...

Fulham Football Club

ESTD 1879

Here is the first half of our star-studded Football A-Z.

There's a player for every letter of the alphabet!

ANSWERS ON PAGE 62

H Played his football for Bundesliga outfit Schalke 04 before arriving at Craven Cottage.

A-Z

K Born in France, but is a Malian international

I He Won the Championship Player of the Year at the Football League Awards earlier this year

L He was named in the England squad for the 2014 FIFA World Cup.

J Australian captain of Crystal Palace and his national team

M He was Forest's longest serving player before his move to the King Power Stadium.

27

30

chris DAVID

Train hard. Play harder!

If you go to every Whites game home and away you'll see the players in action for 90 minutes every weekend and sometimes in mid-week too. That isn't all the players do though. Footballers have to spend a lot of time preparing for matches and afterwards assessing how well they have done with the coaching staff.

Video-analysts have an important role to play. Every player has his performance examined in detail so the player and coaches can build on his strengths and work on developing areas of weakness. This isn't just for first team players but young players too.

Much of the hard work to get players fit comes in pre-season when the squad are likely to do a lot of running and working with weights so that players build up the core strength and stamina they'll need to get them through 46 tough Championship games, cup ties and possibly Play offs at the end of a long gruelling season.

As any player will tell you though, you only get real tip-top match fitness by playing in games. This is why footballers usually only believe they are getting up to their best standard when they have been able to play a few games in a row.

Coaching staff carefully monitor the fitness levels of every player and can give an individual extra work if he needs it. Sometimes coaching staff have to tell a player to rest if he is doing too much because rest and recuperation can be as vital for muscles as time spent in the gym. It's about getting the balance right so the more games there are to play the less time will be spent on fitness work.

Training sessions work on skills, tactics and set piece routines as well with more and more game focus in the days leading up to a fixture.

Fulham
Football Club
ESTᴰ 1879

31

CLUB A:

CLUB B:

CLUB C:

CLUB D:

CLUB E:

CLUB F:

Wild about Footy

CLUB G:

CLUB H:

CLUB I:

CLUB J:

ANSWERS ON PAGE 62

DRILLS: Attacking

Fulham Football Club

ESTD 1879

Set up a square within shooting distance of your goal. Place a keeper in goal, and a defender inside the square.

You and the rest of your mates are attackers and should start at the other side of the square from the goal.

The purpose of this drill is to focus on dribbling to beat a defender and finishing with a shot on goal.

Remember to take turns being in goal so that everyone gets a chance to play all positions!

EASY

Dribble into the square and try to beat the defender and dribble out of the opposite side of the square.

If you successfully dribble through the square without losing the ball to the defender, finish with a shot on goal!

If you lose the ball to the defender or dribble out either side of the square, you must then switch places with the defender so that you are protecting the square and they become an attacker.

The next player in line can go as soon as a shot on goal is taken or the defender has won the ball.

HARD

You can make the square bigger to make it easier for the attackers or make the square smaller to make it easier for the defenders.

HARDER

You can make the square slightly larger and add a second defender so that the game becomes 2 v 1 and harder for the attacker.

To make shooting harder, move the square further away from the goal and encourage a longer shot.

33

Fulham
Football Club
ESTD 1879

...but it's a win over the other team in the Borough of Fulham that is the most satisfying.

DerbyDays

ARTHUR REYNOLDS

MANAGER, PHIL KELSO

FULHAM 1-0 CHELSEA
December 3rd 1910

This was the first ever meeting of the clubs. While Fulham began life in 1879, Chelsea had only come about in 1905 after Fulham declined businessman Gus Mears' offer to move to the new ground he had just taken care of at Stamford Bridge.

35,000 people were shoe-horned into Craven Cottage. The game kicked off in poor light and by full time it was hard to see at all. Whether the failing light had anything to do with Chelsea 'keeper James Molyneux mishandling the ball for the only goal of the game is unknown, not that it would bother Fulham fans now or then. 20 minutes had been played when James Smith fired in a shot that was too hot for Molyneux to hold. It was one of 11 Smith scored that season, but one that is still cherished.

Chelsea also 'scored' - or so they thought. Bob Whittingham beat home 'keeper Arthur Reynolds with a penalty only to be ordered to re-take it as his teammates had encroached. Whittingham failed to score with the re-taken penalty and Reynolds' clean sheet was protected - no Fulham 'keeper has kept clean sheets for four or more games on more occasions than long serving Reynolds.

FULHAM 1-0 CHELSEA
March 19th 2006

Almost a century on from James Smith's winner against Chelsea it was Luis Boa Morte's turn to score the only goal of the game to claim a derby win for the Whites. Chris Coleman's side fought for every ball to win three valuable points which went a long way to ensuring continued membership of the top flight.

It was a feisty affair, a hard-fought victory even by derby game standards. As in 1910 with the re-taken penalty there was controversy. This time the visitors were unhappy about a 59th minute 'goal' disallowed by referee Mike Dean who ruled that Didier Drogba was guilty of handball. The Blues ended with 10 men after the last minute sending off of William Gallas for a foul on Heidar Helguson.

ZAT KNIGHT, IAN PEARCE & LUIS BOA MORTE

GALLAS 13

CHELSEA 2-2 FULHAM

December 30th 2006

CARLOS BOCANEGRA (CENTRE, NEXT TO #13)
CELEBRATES SCORING THE EQUALISER

This was an eventful contest between Fulham and their local rivals.

Moritz Volz gave the Whites an early lead with what was the 15,000th goal scored in the Premiership. Unfortunately just under 20 minutes later Liam Rosenior netted at the wrong end to make it one all at the break.

Just past the hour mark the home side went ahead through Drogba but Fulham's fighting spirit shone through and they deserved the 84th minute equaliser despatched by Carlos Bocanegra.

MORITZ VOLZ CELEBRATES
HIS GOAL WITH LIAM ROSENIOR

FULHAM 3-2 CHELSEA

May 14th 1951

This handsome FA Cup 5th round replay provided Fulham with a famous victory which took them through to a quarter final tie with Blackpool.

Bill Dodgin senior's side had already knocked out Sheffield Wednesday and Millwall before being paired with the Blues at the Bridge. John Campbell had scored the goal that had beaten The Lions in their Den and it was the Irishman whose goal brought about this replay, Roy Bentley having scored for the home side.

Chelsea though would have no reply at the Cottage where a crowd of just under 30,000 saw Fulham storm through with two goals from Bobby Brennan and another from Arthur Stevens leaving Chelsea 'keeper Peter Pickering helpless.

JOHNNY ARNOLD

ARTHUR STEVENS

FULHAM 3 CHELSEA 2

24 February 1936

This goal-laden FA Cup fifth round replay victory was part of a thrilling run to the semi finals. A goalless draw had been earned at Stamford Bridge but whereas defences had been on top in the first game this would be a five goal thriller.

Trevor Smith, Jim Hammond and Johnny Arnold were the goal-scoring heroes, Hammond maintaining his record of scoring in every round. William Barrowclough notched both of Chelsea's strikes but it wasn't enough as a crowd of 30,696 celebrated. Arnold and Smith would be amongst the scorers as Fulham followed up the victory by beating Derby at the Cottage to reach only their second FA Cup semi final and the first since 1908.

1. Which out on loan player starred in the 2014 World Cup in Brazil for Greece?

2. Which Country did Bryan Ruiz represent in the 2014 FIFA World Cup in Brazil?

3. Who scored Fulham's first goal of the season?

4. Which player joined Fulham in a deal that took former left-back Paul Konchesky to Liverpool?

5. Who played alongside Ross McCormack at Elland Road before moving to Craven Cottage?

6. Which current player has played more than 40 times for Colombia?

7. Which Whites star was born in Perth, Australia and represented the Socceroos at the FIFA World Cup in Brazil?

8. What is the name of the Fulham mascot?

9. Which player, at the age of 13, was filmed for a McDonald's advert doing keepy-uppies?

10. Against which Club did Fulham earn their first point of the 2014/15 season?

WHITES
Mastermind

Fulham Football Club
ESTD 1879

1. The Club was born when a school teacher and churchwarden formed a team for local boys. What was the Club's original name?

2. When the Club's name was shortened to Fulham Football Club in 1889, what nickname had to be dropped?

3. Who was the manager when Fulham were Football League Division One Champions in 2001?

4. When Fulham got to the FA Cup final in 1975, who did they beat 1-0 in the semi-final replay?

5. ...and who scored the goal in the last minute of extra time?

6. 2009/10 saw Fulham progress to the Europa League Final, only to be heart-broken by a late extra-time winner from which club?

7. This man is a true Fulham legend. He played a club-record 657 games and scored 157 goals.

8. The top scorer of all time who scored 178 times.

9. Which former England boss enjoyed two spells as a player at Craven Cottage and one as Manager?

10. This footballing legend scored 71 seconds into his debut for the Club.

Art Attack

Fulham
Football Club
ESTᴰ 1879

Can you
finish this
picture of
Scott
Parker?

...and
colour it
in?

STEVE FINNAN

BREDE HANGELAND

Playing at the back is hard! Are you up to the job?

So, if you think you've got what it takes, here are some top tips to get you on your way to becoming a defensive dynamo!

1 **APPLY PRESSURE!**
Badger the attacking side constantly to force them to make mistakes, make life as difficult as you can for them. It's hard to score goals when you're under pressure.

2 **BE ON THE BALL!**
Stay on your toes and be ready to sprint for a stray ball at any time.

3 **MARK YOUR MAN!**
Always know where your attacker is, never let him get behind you or you'll lose sight of the ball.

4 **KEEP YOUR EYES ON THE PRIZE.**
Don't let the ball out of your sight, that way, it can't sneak up on you! Also, watch your attacker's feet to anticipate what they will do.

5 **KEEP IN TOUCH WITH YOUR GOALIE.**
He often has a better view of what is going on on the pitch and will be able to direct you.

6 **DON'T DIVE RECKLESSLY!**
If you haven't got a good view of the ball, don't dive or slide in, you'll only get yourself into bother.

7 **NEVER GIVE UP!**
Keep moving, if an attacker has got past you, go after him, fast!

8 **BE TOUGH!**
Tackle hard and fast, but always go for the ball, not the man.

9 **WATCH THE GAME!**
Always be aware and watch for passes you can intercept.

10 **WORK AS A TEAM!**
If a fellow defender is working on an attacker, be there to support him. You need to be around to provide back-up if the attacker gets past him.

TOP 3: Defenders

Fulham Football Club
ESTD 1879

1956-1969

A true Fulham legend and a one-club man, Cohen amassed 459 appearances for the Whites over 13 years before his career was cut short at 29 due to injury.

A strong right-back who was superb at overlapping and linking up with the midfielder in front of him, Cohen became a stalwart in the Fulham team and later the England side, becoming vice-captain for his country. His most famous moment came when he helped England win their only World Cup in 1966, playing in every game including the Final, where the Three Lions famously beat West Germany 4-2.

The fact remains that England has never won the World Cup without a Fulham player in the team!

George COHEN

Brede HANGELAND

2008-2014

Brede Hangeland joined Fulham in the January transfer window of the 2007/08 season, and promptly helped the side avoid relegation that season, becoming a fixture in the 'Great Escape' team.

A towering figure, Hangeland was almost unbeatable in the air and an excellent tackler and interceptor of the ball. Not only that, he was calm in possession and had great passing ability for a centre-back. He made 270 appearances in his seven years at Craven Cottage, and like Danny Murphy, was ever present in the famous side that reached the UEFA Europa League Final in 2010.

He became Club Captain in 2012 after Murphy's departure.

Roger BROWN
1980-1983

With an absolute no-nonsense style of play, Roger Brown would get stuck in and play without any fear whatsoever every time he stepped out onto the pitch.

Formidable in the air both in defence and at attacking corners, Brown scored an incredible 12 league goals in 46 games in the 1981/82 season - a figure any striker would be happy with! One of those goals was the crucial equaliser against Lincoln City on the final day of the season, securing promotion to Division Two. There's a very famous photo of Brown following that game, celebrating in classic Roger Brown style. Have a look for it!

HONOURABLE MENTIONS: Aaron Hughes, Bobby Moore, Tony Gale, Steve Finnan, Simon Morgan

41

Fulham
Football Club
ESTD 1879

Guess the Club

A.

B.

C.

D.

E.

F.

G.

H.

I.

J.

K.

CAPITAL CITY:
San José

WHERE IS IT: Located in Central America, bordered by Nicaragua to the north, Panama to the southeast, the Pacific Ocean to the west, the Caribbean Sea to the east, and Ecuador to the south of Cocos Island.

FAMOUS COSTA RICANS: Engineer, physicist, and astronaut Franklin Diaz, Chess Grandmaster Alejandro Ramirez, Real Madrid keeper Keylor Navas and Olympic swimmer Claudia Poll.

BRYAN RUIZ

COSTA RICA

Keylor Navas

I'M FROM...

COLOMBIA

COSTA RICA
VENUZUE
COLOMBIA

CAPITAL CITY: Bogotá

WHERE IS IT: Colombia is a country situated in the northwest of South America, bordered to the northwest by Panama; to the east by Venezuela and Brazil; to the south by Ecuador and Peru with an approx population of 47 million.

FAMOUS COLOMBIANS: Singer, songwriter Shakira, Painter and sculptor Fernando Botero, actor John Leguizamo.

Juan Pablo Montoya - race car driver in NASCAR, Formula One and Indycar.

Shakira

HUGO RODALLEGA

MONTENEGRO

MONTENEGRO

Elsad Zverotić

Fulham
Football Club
ESTD 1879

CAPITAL CITY: Podgorica

WHERE IS IT: Montenegro is in Southeastern Europe. It has a coast on the Adriatic Sea to the south-west and is bordered by Croatia to the west, Bosnia and Herzegovina to the north-west, Serbia to the north-east, Kosovo to the east, and Albania to the south-east.

FAMOUS MONTENEGRINS: Prize-winning musician Miloš Karadaglic , performance artist Marina Abramovic and former Red Star Belgrade and A.C. Milan star Dejan Savicevic.

Patricia Velasquez

VENEZUELA

WHERE IS IT: Venezuela is on the northern coast of South America and its territory covers around 916,445 square km with an estimated population of approximately 29,100,000.

CAPITAL CITY: Caracas

FAMOUS VENEZUELANS: Actress Patricia Velasquez, Model Dayana Mendoza and former rugby union footballer Serge Blanco.

FERNANDO AMOREBIETA

Fulham Football Club

ESTD 1879

Who would you sign for the Whites?

DESIGN A Star PLAYER

Imagine you wanted to sign a new central midfielder. Look at the qualities listed here and choose the main ones you'd like the Fulham scouts out looking for.

List all of the qualities here in order with your most important quality as number one, the second most important thing as number two and so on. When you've done that estimate how much you'd be prepared to spend on the player you have identified.

You can also write the name of the player - in the Football League, Premier League or from elsewhere - that you think most fits the description you've come up with.

HEADING
He has to be able to head the ball like **MATT SMITH**

STAMINA
He has to have a 'good engine' like **KONSTANTINOS STAFYLIDIS**

SKILL
He has to have quick feet and tricks like **PATRICK ROBERTS**

SHOOTING
He has to be able to shoot like **ROSS McCORMACK**

VERSATILITY
He has to be able to play in more than one position like **TIM HOOGLAND**

SHORT PASSING
He has to be able to keep possession like **EMERSON HYNDMAN**

CROSSING
He has to be able to cross the ball like **KONSTANTINOS STAFYLIDIS**

LONG PASSING
He has to be able to hit sweeping passes like **CHRIS DAVID**

TACKLING
He has to be able to tackle like **SCOTT PARKER**

ATTITUDE
He has to have a good attitude like **CAULEY WOODROW**

	SKILL	PLAYER	PRICE
1			
2			
3			
4			
5			
6			
7			
8			
9			
10			

cauley WOODROW

Have your mates form a circle around you, everyone facing you. You have the ball.

EASY

Throw the ball towards the other players' heads in turn, as if they are going to head the ball.

While the ball is in the air, shout 'HEAD' or 'CATCH' to whoever you are directing the ball to. The player must then quickly react to your command and perform the task you have shouted.

This drill is supposed to be fun! You will be working on your heading and reaction skills without even realising it!

Make sure to take turns being the player in the middle!

If you yelled 'HEAD' the player must head the ball back to you.

If you yelled 'CATCH' the player must catch the ball and return it.

If a player performs the wrong task, that player sits and only standing players are still in the game. The last player standing wins the round.

HARD

To make this drill more difficult, have the players do the opposite task to what you have shouted, e.g. if you shout 'CATCH' they must 'HEAD' the ball.

Also start throwing the ball to players randomly, keeping everyone on their toes as they don't know whose turn will be next!

HARDER

To develop this drill further, you can introduce other tasks - volley, chest trap or catch with your knees.

Can you think of any more to add?

P Tough tackling midfielder who has represented England at every level from U16 to senior.

Q Irish midfielder, made over 200 appearances for Sheffield United

R A young forward who came through Burnley's youth ranks

STAR STUDDE

N Scored his 50th league goal for the Foxes last season helping secure promotion to the Premier League

S An extremely quick player who represented his country at the 2012 Olympics and the 2014 FIFA World Cup.

O Finished the 2014 FIFA World Cup with 15 chances created, the most of any German player

T He was voted African Player of the Year for 2011, 2012 and 2013.

Figure out who's who...

Here is the second half of our star-studded Football A-Z.

There's a player for every letter of the alphabet!

ANSWERS ON PAGE 62

U Recently returned to Argentina to play for Newell's Old Boys

A-Z

X First player in FC Barcelona's history to play 150 international matches

 **V** Received the Players' Player of the Season Award last term with Leicester City

 **Y** Started his career at Watford and has now made over sixty appearances for Manchester United

W In 2011, while at Luton Town, he became the first non-League footballer to play for an England youth team since 1974.

Z Born in the Ivory Coast, he made his debut for England in 2012

CAPITAL CITY: Stockholm

SWEDEN

Alexander Kačaniklić

WHERE IS IT: Sweden is a Scandinavian country in Northern Europe which borders Norway and Finland, and is connected to Denmark by a bridge-tunnel across the Oresund.

At 450,295 square km (173,860 sq miles), Sweden is the third largest country in the European Union by area, with a total population of about 9.6 million.

FAMOUS SWEDES: Film actor Dolph Lundgren, Ingvar Kamprad, the founder of IKEA, tennis legend, Bjorn Borg and Swedish DJ, remixer and record producer Tim Bergling, better known as Avicii.

Avicii

FINLAND

SWEDEN

GREECE

I'M FROM...

GREECE

CAPITAL CITY: Athens

WHERE IS IT: Greece is a country in Southern Europe.

It borders Albania to the north-west, Macedonia and Bulgaria to the north and Turkey to the north-east.

Greece has a population of around 11 million.

FAMOUS GREEKS: Philosopher Socrates, philosopher and scientist Aristotle,

Academy Award-winning composer Vangelis and rock musician Tommy Lee.

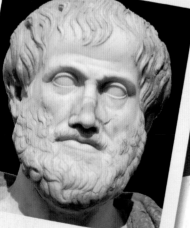

Aristotle

KONSTANTINOS STAFYLIDIS

FINLAND

Fulham
Football Club
ESTᴰ 1879

JESSE JORONEN

AUSTRALIA

AUSTRALIA

WHERE IS IT:
Finland is a Nordic country situated in the Fennoscandian region of Northern Europe, bordered by Sweden to the west, Norway to the north, Russia to the east, and Estonia to the south across the Gulf of Finland.

It is the eighth largest country in Europe in terms of area and has a population of around 5.5 million.

FAMOUS FINNS: Long-distance runner Lasse Viren, winner of four gold medals at the 1972 and 1976 Summer Olympics, tennis ace Jarkko Nieminen, composer Jean Sibelius and actor Peter Franzén.

Hugh Jackman

CAPITAL CITY:
Canberra

WHERE IS IT: Australia is a country comprising of the mainland of the Australian continent, the island of Tasmania, and numerous smaller islands. It is the world's sixth-largest country by total area with a population of approx 24 million.

FAMOUS AUSTRALIANS: Actor Hugh Jackman, Pop star and actress Kylie Minogue, INXS rock star Michael Hutchence and legendary cricketer Donald Bradman.

ADAM TAGGART

Fulham
Football Club
ESTD 1879

WHO ARE

A

- Born in Aberdeen but moved to Australia
- Played in Celtic's and Aberdeen's youth teams
- Highly rated in Australia, where he was playing senior football for ECU Joondalup

B

At Luton he became the first non-League player capped at youth level for England since the '70s

Spent half of last term on loan at Southend Utd

An England U21 international

C

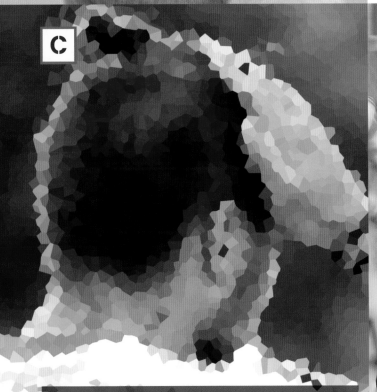

On a season-long loan from Bundesliga side Bayer Leverkusen

Started his career in Greece with PAOK

Greek U17, U19, U20, U21 & Full international

D

- His youth career began at Swedish club Helsingborg before joining Liverpool
- Has had loan spells at Watford and Burnley
- A Swedish international

YER

E

Born on 12 July 1996 in Pontoise, France

Signed for Fulham aged sixteen
from Paris Saint-Germain

Made his Premier League debut on
30 November 2013 against West Ham

A:

B:

C:

D:

E:

F:

Mascot Mania

G:

H:

I:

J:

Fulham
Football Club
ESTD 1879

Nikolay BODUROV

6

Being a keeper is a tough job...

Fulham
Football Club
ESTD 1879

...but someone's got to do it!

EDWIN VAN DER SAR

ANTTI NIEMI

TOP 10 GOALKEEPING TIPS

So, if you think you're man enough for the challenge, here are some top tips to get you on track for becoming an all star 'keeper!

1 KEEP MOVING AND STAY ON YOUR TOES!
A good goalie's feet are constantly moving and ready for anything that's coming their way. Never sit back on your heels, that's when you'll make mistakes.

2 SHOUT... LOUD!
You have to communicate with your team, let them know when you need help or when you think they need to be watching opposing players.

3 STAY LOOSE AND RELAXED.
If you're tense, diving and getting hit with the ball will hurt more.

4 STAY AWAKE!
You've got to be watching the game all the time in order to be ready to step up when it's your turn to shine. Remember, it only takes seconds for the game to change completely.

5 WATCH PLAYERS' FEET.
The way their feet are positioned when going to take a kick can indicate where the ball is going.

6 BOUNCE BACK!
After diving your length for a ball, recover quickly, play doesn't stop because you're on the ground.

7 STAY SQUARE TO THE BALL.
At all times, keep your hips and shoulders pointed towards the shooter.

8 TREAT ALL SHOTS WITH RESPECT!
No matter how soft the shot or how easy the save, always make the effort to get the ball under full control. It's when you get lazy that mistakes happen.

9 HAVE AN INSURANCE POLICY!
Always have a part of your body behind the ball as well as your hands. That way, if the ball slips through your fingers, your body will be there to stop it.

10 HAVE COURAGE!
Take pride in your position as your team's last defender and have confidence in yourself. You have to put yourself in positions where you might end up getting hit but it's these saves that win matches.

TOP 3: Goalkeepers

Mark SCHWARZER

2008-2013

Mark Schwarzer joined Fulham on a free transfer from Middlesbrough in the summer of 2008.

Named the Club's Player of the Year at the end of his first campaign at Craven Cottage, the Australian impressed again the following term, before playing a key role in Fulham's run to the UEFA Europa League final in 2010. The veteran would soon pass the 200-appearance mark in a Whites shirt and also earned 109 caps for his country. He hung up his boots on the international scene in 2013 shortly after leaving the Whites on a free transfer for London rivals Chelsea.

In his first season at Stamford Bridge, he played in the UEFA Champions League Semi-Final.

Edwin VAN DER SAR

2001-2005

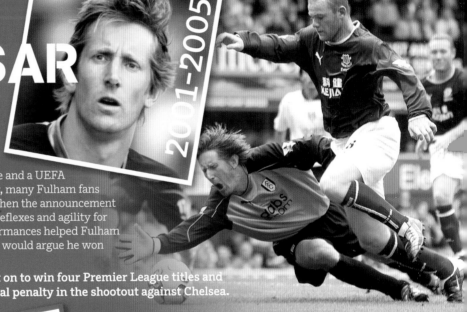

When Edwin van der Sar joined Fulham for £7.1m during the Mohamed Al Fayed revolution in 2001 it was a sign that the Whites were really going places.

One of the best goalkeepers in the world at the time and a UEFA Champions League and multiple Eredivisie winner, many Fulham fans would be forgiven for their jaws hitting the floor when the announcement of the signing was made! A goalkeeper with great reflexes and agility for such a huge figure, his consistently excellent performances helped Fulham establish themselves in the Premier League - some would argue he won us points almost single handedly at times.

Moved to Manchester United in 2005 and went on to win four Premier League titles and the Champions League again - saving the crucial penalty in the shootout against Chelsea.

Tony MACEDO

1955-1968

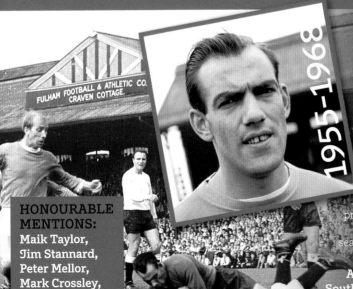

Inconsistent but brilliant on his day, for many older supporters, Gibraltar-born Tony Macedo was the best-ever Fulham goalkeeper.

Joined Fulham as a 16-year-old junior in 1954 and was on national service in Germany when Manager Dug Livingstone called him into the first team in December 1958. He was a regular thereafter for a decade, making 391 appearances. Brave, acrobatic and spectacular, Macedo was, in the best continental tradition of goalkeepers, also prone to the occasional lapse. But he was an integral part of the successes of those years as two FA Cup Semi-Finals, promotion in 1959 and nine seasons of top-flight football proved. Although Macedo played 10 times for the England Under-23s, he missed out on the full cap he deserved.

After a season (1968/69) with Colchester United, Macedo went to South Africa to finish his playing career and eventually settled there.

HONOURABLE MENTIONS:
Maik Taylor,
Jim Stannard,
Peter Mellor,
Mark Crossley,
Antti Niemi

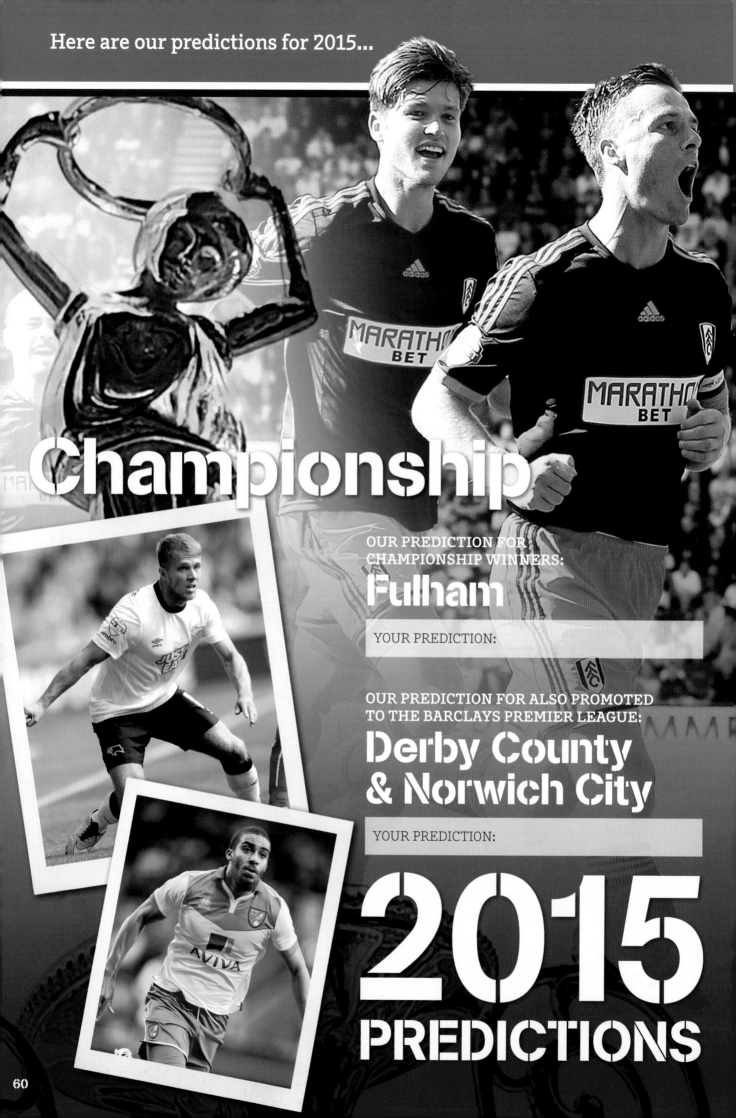

Championship

OUR PREDICTION FOR
CHAMPIONSHIP WINNERS:

Fulham

YOUR PREDICTION:

OUR PREDICTION FOR ALSO PROMOTED
TO THE BARCLAYS PREMIER LEAGUE:

Derby County & Norwich City

YOUR PREDICTION:

2015
PREDICTIONS

Premier League

Fulham
Football Club
ESTᴅ 1879

OUR PREDICTION FOR BARCLAYS
PREMIER LEAGUE CHAMPIONS:
Arsenal

YOUR PREDICTION:

OUR PREDICTION FOR
BARCLAYS PREMIER
LEAGUE RUNNERS UP:
Chelsea

YOUR PREDICTION:

OUR PREDICTION FOR BARCLAYS
PREMIER LEAGUE BOTTOM THREE:
Hull City, QPR & Stoke City

YOUR PREDICTION:

OUR PREDICTION FOR FA CUP WINNERS
Liverpool

YOUR PREDICTION:

Fulham Football Club

ESTD 1879

Answers

PAGE 22: FAN'TASTIC
Andy Murray, Lewis Hamilton, Bradley Wiggins, David Beckham and Rory McIlroy.

PAGE 24: BILLY'S SUMS
1. 44. 2. 21. 3. 6. 4. 21. 5. 26. 6. 32. 7. 5. 8. 3

PAGE 26: STAR STUDDED A-Z PART 1
A. Fernando Amorebieta. B. Craig Bryson. C. Nathaniel Chalobah.
D. Moussa Dembélé E. Marvin Emnes. F. George Friend.
G. Olivier Giroud. H. Tim Hoogland. I. Danny Ings. J. Mile Jedinak.
K. Jimmy Kébé. L. Rickie Lambert. M. Wes Morgan.

PAGE 29. FACE OFF
A. Cameron Burgess. B. Tim Hoogland. C. Cauley Woodrow.
D. Patrick Roberts. E. Scott Parker. F. Kay Voser. G. Chris David.
H. Ross McCormack. I. Moussa Dembélé.

PAGE 32: WILD ABOUT FOOTY
A. Sunderland. B. Derby County. C. Norwich City.
D. Sheffield Wednesday. E. Hull City. F. Watford.
G. Wolverhampton Wanderers. H. Newcastle United.
I. Leicester City. J. Millwall.

PAGE 36: WHITES MASTERMIND - FOR THE KIDS
1. Konstantinos Mitroglou. 2. Costa Rica. 3. Tim Hoogland.
4. Alex Kačaniklić. 5. Matt Smith. 6. Hugo Rodallega.
7. Adam Taggart. 8. Billy the Badger. 9. Scott Parker.
10. Cardiff City.

PAGE 37: WHITES MASTERMIND - FOR THE OLDIES
1. Fulham St Andrew's. 2. The Saints. 3. Jean Tigana.
4. Birmingham City. 5. John Mitchell. 6. Atletico Madrid.
7. Johnny Haynes. 8. Gordon Davies. 9. Bobby Robson.
10. George Best.

PAGE 42:
GUESS THE CLUB
A. Brighton & Hove
Albion. B. Ipswich Town.
C. Middlesbrough.
D. Sheffield Wednesday.
E. Nottingham Forest. F. Derby
County. G. Bolton Wanderers.
H. Wolverhampton Wanderers. I. Norwich City.
J. Birmingham City. K. Blackburn Rovers.

PAGE 50: STAR STUDDED A-Z PART 2
N. David Nugent. O. Mesut Özil. P. Scott Parker.
Q. Stephen Quinn. R. Jay Rodriguez. S. Daniel Sturridge.
T. Yaya Touré. U. Óscar Ustari. V. Jamie Vardy.
W. Cauley Woodrow. X. Xavi. Y. Ashley Young. Z. Wilfried Zaha.

PAGE 54: WHO ARE YER?
A. Cameron Burgess. B. Cauley Woodrow. C. Kostas Stafylidis.
D. Alexander Kačaniklić. E. Moussa Dembele.

PAGE 56: MASCOT MANIA
A. Gully, Brighton & Hove Albion. B. Barney Owl, Sheffield
Wednesday. C. Bloomfield Bear, Blackpool. D. Kop Cat, Leeds
United. E. Rover the Dog, Blackburn Rovers. F. Robin Hood,
Nottingham Forest. G. Captain Canary, Norwich City. H. Floyd,
Charlton Athletic. I. Beau Brummie, Birmingham City. J. Lofty
the Lion, Bolton Wanderers.